Praise for

Off With His Head

'Funny and cleverly written, this is the future of history that should be told'

KATIE KENNEDY,

The History Gossip and author of *Was Anne of Cleves a Minger? and 365 Other Historical Curiosities*

'A clever, tongue-in-cheek guide for modern women who don't mind getting a little medieval when it comes to punting a jerk back to the manosphere from whence he came'

NICOLE TERSIGNI,

author of *Men to Avoid in Art and Life*

'Vicious and delicious. Coles has crafted a manual that is at once hilarious and educational'

KYLE PRUE,

author of *How to Piss Off Men*

Off With His Head

100 Medieval Methods to Silence a Man (for good)

MEGAN COLES

Tallis Street

First published in 2026 by Tallis Street Books
An imprint of Headline Publishing Group Limited

1

Cataloguing in Publication Data is available from the British Library.

Hardback ISBN 978 1 0354 3906 5

Typeset by EM&EN
Printed and bound in Great Britain by Clays Ltd, Elcograf S.p.A.

Headline's policy is to use papers that are natural, renewable and recyclable products and made from wood grown in well-managed forests and other controlled sources. The logging and manufacturing processes are expected to conform to the environmental regulations of the country of origin.

Headline Publishing Group Limited
An Hachette UK Company
Carmelite House
50 Victoria Embankment
London EC4Y 0DZ

The authorised representative in the EEA is Hachette Ireland,
8 Castlecourt Centre, Dublin 15, D15 XTP3, Ireland (email: info@hbgi.ie)

www.headline.co.uk
www.hachette.co.uk

INTRODUCTION

Dearest modern women,

Today, you find yourselves faced with endless choices. Avocado on your bagel or smoked salmon? Cocktails at home or clubbing with your girlies? And do you think it's better to block that walking red flag you've been speaking to or just silently ghost him?

When a guy gives us the ick, we can unmatch him on whatever heinous dating app he crawled out of and then laugh about it with our besties over a glass of wine. But back in times of olde, in order to get rid of a man, women had to get a little more creative. And thus, I proudly present to you *Off With His Head: 100 Ways to Silence a Man (for good)*, where you can take inspiration from women of bygone days who wished to put a stop to the fuckwittage of knaves and manwenches alike.

From mysterious accidents to cunningly orchestrated catastrophes, it turns out that, historically, women probably did a lot more than just poison their misbehaving husbands.

We are much smarter than that, after all.

DEATH BY Uncontrollable laughter

'MEN DON'T rate women for funniness,' they say when you turn up to the joust dressed as a cocktail olive.

Me personally? I jest too much. Force-feed him an entire goose ('No, babe, that paltock doesn't make you look fat!') and crack a joke. He'll *die* laughing.

DEATH BY
Rug

YE OLDE fuckboy cheated on you with sketty Sarah from the next village? Hark! Fear not. Bring a bestie and – instead of throwing glitter all over his carpet and keying his car – roll that man up in a rug and 'accidentally' leave him in the path of a herd of horses.

It'll be like Ascot. Except, y'know . . . with more screaming.

DEATH BY Wine

NOW, I love a piss-up as much as the next wench but sometimes the boysies take it too far.

First it's all, 'Oh, I'm just having a couple of pints of mead with the fellas,' and the next thing you know, he's waking up in ye olde Benidorm with Eleanor of Aquitaine's hair extensions wrapped around his John Thomas.

Tell him that submerging himself in a barrel of malmsey wine for four hours will do wonders for his receding hairline and he won't do that again in a hurry. (Note: This may take longer if he wants to get out and use the toilet.)

DEATH BY

Autoerotic asphyxiation

YOUR FELLA keeps his hat and tights on during sex *and* he won't go down on you? Why not suggest a touch of autoerotic asphyxiation to spice things up in the bedroom? You get to strangle him to death; he dies with a massive stonk on. It's a win–win.

DEATH BY Sneezing

NOTHING pisses me off more than a loud man-sneeze. Who does he think he is, the town crier?

Gently encourage him to hold it in. You won't get the ick again – because he'll be dead.

DEATH BY
Lampreys

'AND FOR the lady? Perhaps a salad?' he says as he sits there stuffing his gob with an entire leg of roast ham.

Haha. Perhaps not.

Order a surfeit of lampreys and, because he's a great, tyrannical pie shop on legs who doesn't like seeing a woman who isn't full after consuming half a pickled egg, he will inevitably eat the lot himself. With any luck, he'll pull a Henry I.

DEATH BY
Boiling oil

IF HE SAYS anything other than 'Yea' to your inane 'Wouldst thou still loveth me if I were a worm?', he deserves to feel death's gentle caress.

Take him on a little day trip to London's Smithfield to watch the coin clippers and porridge poisoners boil in oil (fun for all the family). A gentle nudge while he's peering over the edge of the vat and he'll end up resembling a Cup-a-Soup.

DEATH BY
Lute

IS HE ONE OF those street interviewers who badgers fair maidens in the town with inane questions like 'Would ye cheat on your man for twenty shillings?' in the hopes of going viral on ye olde wretched clock app? Yeah, that would make me drier than a monk's wine cellar, too.

Encourage him to start playing the lute to help lure unsuspecting women to him for questioning. Little does he know the instrument you're gifting him has experienced a little wear and tear, and a splinter-related injury that is destined to go septic awaits.

DEATH BY
Boner

IF HE'S MORE interested in scrolling through OnlyWenches than giving you a good seeing to, obviously there are some issues going on in the trouser-snake department. So why not offer him some Spanish Fly as a little titbit? A popular – yet deadly – aphrodisiac used in many a love potion, this will make him stiff (but not in the way he might like).

DEATH BY Throne

IMAGINE BEING told not to eat for three days by a man with C-cup breasts and a codpiece the size of a cornichon.

Plonk Mr Big Titties on a rickety wooden throne and, with the blessing of womankind, the entire structure will collapse beneath him. If the floor happens to be made from stone, he probably won't get back up again.

DEATH BY Mansplaining

PICTURE THIS: you're on a first date at the local Wetherspoons tavern. You matched with this guy on ye olde Tyn'dre around a week ago and, sure, he didn't ask you many questions about yourself, but at least he seemed funny.

Now, he's yapping for England. Frankly, nobody wants to hear about the fact that he would have been a jousting champion if it wasn't for his knee injury. And him (unnecessarily) correcting you – very slowly and loudly, as though you're not even capable of milking a cow – on who won the Battle of Agincourt is becoming very grating. But if he mansplains for long enough, there is a slim chance that he may starve to death. All you need to do is smile and nod, since he won't let you get a word in anyway.

DEATH BY
Chess

SO HE THINKS he's cleverer than you just because he's a man? Show him who *really* wears the tights and challenge the smug little toerag to a game of chess, then stress him out so much (while you beat his arse) that he has a stroke.

I call that women in male fields.

DEATH BY
Lead

IT'S ALWAYS the broke manwenches who are worried about the woman they're dating being a gold digger. Take him out for a nice expensive meal (he's so used to scoffing pottage and the McDungeon's Saver Menu that he'll inevitably order everything smothered in gold leaf). Then, when he pops to the loo, sprinkle a little powdered white lead across his plate.

Knowing him, he'll probably think it's Parmesan.

DEATH BY
Bacon

DID YOUR girls make fun of you because they saw your boyfriend doing cringy dances on ye olde clock app . . . unironically? The levels of ick must be off the Richter scale.

Encourage him to have a boogie a little *too close* to the fireplace – where you have, conveniently, hung an enormous flitch of bacon to smoke. All his jigging about should cause the rope suspending the bacon to snap, leaving him resembling a squashed cabbage.

DEATH BY

Orange peel

HE TOLD YOU OFF for saying 'cunny' on the first date and now you're about to ask the tavern wench for Angela? Hark! Fear not, for I have a better idea.

Yes, yes – I know an orange is worth its weight in gold but hear me out: eat it on the sly and discard the skin somewhere near his absurdly long shoes. If he slips, he'll (fingers crossed) develop a nasty case of gangrene and pop his clogs.

DEATH BY

Botched escape

AFTER HE'S exhausted himself thinking he's performed valiantly in the bedroom, offer to fetch Sir Top Shagger a glass of water. He'll be so busy flexing in the mirror, he won't notice that you've taken the key and locked him in, leaving him no choice but to exit via the window.

Supply him with enough bedsheets, and I can guarantee he'll tie them together and try to escape. A *very* nasty fall awaits . . .

DEATH BY Cake

DISCOVERED him in Azure the Fair's queue of 1,000 men? I think a touch of public humiliation should put a stop to his shenanigans.

When he trots down to church on Palm Sunday, secretly join the local children in their funny little tradition of throwing cakes at the congregation from the church roof (just make sure to lob a particularly stale one at his temple for good measure).

DEATH BY

Footstool

NOBODY LIKES a sentient peanut that moans about 'females' 25/8 and brags about how many wenches he's clapped in Southwark's stewes. Your best bet is to entice him into letting you use him as a human footstool by promising you'll watch ye olde sheep racing with him. He'll die of exhaustion, and you get to stuff him and leave him resembling a misshapen turnip.

Truly, you'd be doing *all* of womankind a favour (and saving quite a few of us a syphilis diagnosis).

DEATH BY
Stake

HE WON'T let you wear your favourite kirtle because he thinks it's too low-cut? BURN HIM.

No, I'm serious. Tell the Bishop that he's been spotted canoodling with the local witch and he'll have him tied to a stake (and resembling a scrumptious Flat Iron wagyu) before you can say, 'I bite my thumb at thee, thou great hairy cunny.'

DEATH BY

The Duke of Exeter's daughter

WE HAVE ALL encountered a man who has lied about his height on OkCrossbowman, unfortunately. But fear not, baddies, wenches and witches alike, for the Duke of Exeter's daughter exists for a reason.

Fool him into thinking that it's a brand-new contraption that will spice things up in the bedroom, then simply secure his wrists and ankles to the rack and turn the handle, trying not to jump for joy as his joints dislocate and he screams in agony. But, hey – at least he'll be a few inches taller!

DEATH BY
Iron maiden

NOBODY LIKES to receive unsolicited illustrations of a man's old boy roaming wild and free out of its unnecessarily oversized codpiece. So why not introduce him to the iron maiden? (And no, I am not talking about your dad's favourite heavy metal minstrels.)

Encourage him into the seemingly innocuous human-shaped cabinet by promising to grab a few snaps of him looking cool for ye olde Insta-Gramme, then slam the door shut. The result? Him taking a million pricks (oo-er) from the spikes within.

DEATH BY

Communion wafer

HE EXPECTS you to split the bill but he can afford to subscribe to OnlyWenches? In the bin. Now.

Send him to church to confess to ye olde sin of lust, where he will (with the blessing of womankind) choke to death on a communion wafer.

DEATH BY Stag

NOTHING GIVES one the ick quite like a man picking up a leaf from the ground and blowing his nose into it. Maid Marion wouldn't put up with that, so why should you?

On his next hunt, encourage him to show off how much of a big, strong alpha male he is ('But babe, *all* the high-value men are doing this nowadays. It says so on ye olde podcasts!') by getting up close and personal with a stag. I can guarantee he'll get dragged to death after getting his belt caught in its antlers.

DEATH BY

Gibbet cage

SO HE HIRED an entire workshop full of scribes to illustrate pictures from your Insta-Gramme so he could plaster them all over his bedroom wall after just *two dates*? Yeah, that ain't right.

The only correct punishment for a man with a penchant for parasocial relationships is a touch of gibbetting. Entice the perv into a cage with promises of Dior Sauvage – or whatever the Hell men like nowadays – and leave him to rot in the public eye.

DEATH BY

Milk and honey

HE HALF-HEARTEDLY washes out sheep gut condoms and uses them with other birds? That's a nasty dose of clap just waiting to happen.

Seduce him into the bedroom with promises of food play and a set of fluffy pink handcuffs, then spoon-feed him so much milk and honey (preferably while the dulcet tones of ye olde Marvin Gaye play in the background) that his IBS kicks in. Smear even more honey across his face, then sit back and relax as every insect in the vicinity rocks up for dinner.

DEATH BY

Cricket ball

A MAN WHO keepeth a list of all the women he's slept with on his Notes app and boasteth of it maketh me, um . . . sicketh.

Encourage him to participate in that good ol' Anglo-Saxon pastime and, provided he's not the sporty type, he might be fortunate enough to receive a surprise cricket ball to the head.

DEATH BY
Exploding bladder

THERE IS nothing quite so grotesque as witnessing your date slurp the meat off twenty chicken bones at the Peri-Peri Pottage House, then pick his teeth with his fingernails.

As much as you may never want to see him again after that, keep him talking for long enough (ask him why we can't 'just mint more coins') and he'll forget to leave the table to pee, resulting in – you guessed it! – a bladder that goes BOOM.

DEATH BY

Poisoned arrow

WHY IS your boyfriend chatting up the local nuns? He is going to cause Sister Assumpta and Sister Agnes *irreparable* trauma.

Next time he's doing a 'lads on tour'-style boar hunt, invite yourself along. Introduce a winning combination of your abysmal aim ('I'm just a girl') and the arrow being poisoned (shock, horror), and he won't know what hit him.

DEATH BY
Catapult

I HATE IT when men try to mansplain how a catapult works to me. Show him just how hands-on you are and organise a practical demonstration! (Bonus points if you manage to send him flying into a vat of pig shit.)

DEATH BY
Pear

MEN SHOULD be seen and not heard, so why not introduce him to the Pear of Anguish™?

With a simple twist, our little friend is designed to expand in the mouth and split the jaw clean open. A popular alternative consists of bending him over and ramming it where the sun don't shine (and I'm not talking about Preston).

Convince him it's a brand-new, state-of-the-art sex toy and I'm sure he'll be down. We don't kink-shame here.

DEATH BY
Olive

THERE IS nothing I hate more than a performative male – and by that I mean someone who paints his nails and reads his truly terrible verse out loud at the local tavern in the hope of making the maidens swoon.

Under the guise of being a kind, generous soul (pretend you're not praying for the downfall of men for a second), order a dinky dish of olives to his table. Choking to death on a toothpick lodged in one of them will save us all from his pseudo-feminist slam poetry.

DEATH BY

Appendix

HOW TO piss off an Englishwoman 101: insist that England is actually part of France. And we all know a man *loves* to play Devil's advocate, especially when they hail from that gaff that Chris Columbus recently stumbled upon.

Convince him that men who eat veggies give you the ick and a touch of constipation will hopefully cause his appendix to explode.

DEATH BY

Lintel

JUST BECAUSE he's part of the Knights Templar does *not* make up for the fact that he's only 4'11 (I know, jacked military guys are hot. Get over yourself). I encourage you to coax him into a game of hide-and-seek in a house with very low ceilings. Play your cards right and he should crack his head on a lintel.

DEATH BY

Flagellation

LET'S BE HONEST: plague was probably caused by your fella wandering around in a slutty little paltock and tights (at least, that's what our icon and legend John of Reading says). So, why not encourage him to become a flagellant? Not only will this spice things up in the bedroom but, if all goes as planned, his welts will go septic and he'll pass away from exhaustion.

DEATH BY

Bear (sort of)

CAUGHT HIM looking at elaborately illustrated titty pics that were doodled by a very bored and randy monk? My suggestion would be to dress up as a bear and chase him with an axe. If you don't hit him, a heart attack will.

DEATH BY

Beheading

YOU KNOW that anal sex is a capital offence, right? So next time he starts whining about how you never let him smash in ye olde back door, grass him up to the king. When the executioner finally manages to hack through his neck and grasps his hair to brandish his head to the crowd, his toupee will come clean off.

DEATH BY
Beard

I'M MORE OF a moustache girl, personally, but if you hype up his beard enough, it might just grow to a suitable length for him to trip over it.

(Double damage: Persuade him to wear a pair of those ridiculously long shoes while you're at it, seeing as he wants to be a court jester so badly.)

DEATH BY
Ducking

NOW, YOU'LL KNOW he's lying because his lips move, but a popular test involves popping the perfidious shitbag on a cucking stool. (I just *know* he'll think you're talking about that lone chair that sits in the corner of your hotel room and his arse will be in that seat quicker than you can say, 'Come out, ye cuckold.')

Little does he know that ducking is a popular practice used to weed out witches and dishonest tradesmen. If he floats, he's a liar, if he sinks . . . Well. He's dead.

DEATH BY
Molehill

YOUR MAN spends all his time out hunting with the boys? Send his horse careering into the path of a molehill. Next thing you know, he's got a broken collarbone and he's on his deathbed with pneumonia (you know how dramatic these men get).

DEATH BY
Toilet

HIS FRIENDS hate you because you don't like him spending every waking hour down the tavern? Fear not, for a conveniently flimsy floor could collapse beneath their feet and send them all tumbling into the lavatory pit below.

Since they enjoy talking shit so much, why not let them drown in it?

DEATH BY
Toilet (option two)

YE OLDE wasteman getting on your last nerve? I'm not surprised – he literally listens to Sir Joeceus Roganov's sermons.

Prithee, I beseech thee: hire a friendly assassin to lurk in the very depths of the bog and then stab him up the jacksie the moment he drops his drawers. Believe me, you'd be doing us *all* a favour.

DEATH BY

Indigestion

A MAN WHO tells you to lay off the sweetmeats because you are getting 'too buxom' isn't a real man, in my opinion.

Take him out for dinner and while he insists you feast upon a lettuce leaf, he will – of course, because he is a hypocritical git – order half the menu, alongside fourteen desserts. But this is all part of your cunning plan because if the indigestion doesn't kill him, vacuuming up the food so fast that he inhales it into his lungs surely will.

DEATH BY

Dancing plague

YOU KNOW what the dancing plague of 1518 and your stinking ex have in common?

They're both bops.

Take him to a rave at the local tavern and he can have a touch of demonic possession as a little treat. (Note: *Please* discourage him from wearing a bucket hat and a bumbag. Nobody wants to see that.)

DEATH BY
Bird

ANY MAN who still uses ye olde Snapchat over the age of twenty-five is a walking ick. Let's be honest: he's probably cheating on you.

Convince him that shaving his head will make him look more virile and have all the village's maidens lifting their skirts. He'll most likely end up resembling an egg and, with any luck, it'll attract a flock of (very maternal) birds who are intent upon clawing his scalp clean off.

DEATH BY

Bed sheets

HE'S WHINGED about you not being enough of a freak in the sheets for *yonks* and to that I say: PROVE THAT KNAVE WRONG.

Wrap him up in your least favourite bed linen, douse it with alcohol and (stay with me now . . .) leave him a little *too close* to an enthusiastically burning candle.

(Top tip: Celebrate with a shot of ale at the Pink Pony Inn with your girlies afterwards.)

DEATH BY
Mercury

'BABE, we've eaten chicken and rice *every night* this week. Do you think we could, I don't know . . . order Burger Kingdom instead?'

Since he insists upon it for his so-called gains, try mixing a little mercury into the chicken feed. At least the meat will actually have some semblance of seasoning when he eats it.

DEATH BY

Syphilis

SINCE YOUR cheating ex wants to be ran through so much, why not coax him into the local stewe? Let's hope he catches a nasty dose of syphilis and his nose will fall off. If that fails, casually bring up the fact that running down the stairs backwards is the hottest new cure for the dreaded French pox. A broken neck awaits . . .

DEATH BY
Turnip

I DON'T KNOW who needs to hear this, but a man recruiting you for OnlyWenches, like some kind of glorified Bishop of Winchester, is not a compliment.

Next time he goes rabbit hunting with the boysies, *please* find a way to position a stray turnip in the path of his horse. The ideal result: he'll be thrown headfirst into a tree.

DEATH BY

Unpoisoned food

PESTERING a girl for gilded illustrations of her knockers is enough to give anyone the ick. Make very loud and repetitive jokes about poisoning his food and he'll be so paranoid, he'll never eat again.

DEATH BY Snakes

THE MARK of an ill-mannered man is one that goes to the bar, orders a mead for himself and sweet FA for his date. Can't be having that, can we?

Entice him into a pit of snakes ('No, babe – I swear they're just gummy worms. What do you mean, "They're moving"?') and he won't do that again in a hurry.

DEATH BY Banquet

NOTHING gets my goat more than a man who lies about fighting the French at Agincourt just to get in my knickers. He thinks I'm a mug? That's OK; she who laughs last, laughs . . . uh, last.

Take him out for dinner (McDungeon's will probably do) and tell him you're paying. He'll eat enough chicken nuggets to sink a battleship and his stomach will explode. Winner winner, chicken dinner.

DEATH BY

Spanish donkey

SO HE MAKES YOU go into another bedchamber to finish yourself off? Ick.

Might I suggest a spell on the Spanish donkey? Simply offer him a seat on this torture device for us maidens of yore next time he comes over to yours for Scrollflix and chill. Chances are he's too stupid to notice quite how narrow it is or the pain it'll inflict on his backside.

(Downside: If he is split in half, that means you *technically* have to put up with two of him.)

DEATH BY

Beer

A MAN WHO reeketh of ale and onions is not a man I want going anywhere near my nether regions.

Disguise a vat of boiling beer as a relaxing bath, complete with a foamy tower of bubbles and little rubber duckies. Just, y'know . . . don't check the temperature before he gets in.

DEATH BY Cock ring

SO HE DOESN'T LIKE you being a right comely wench of ye olde Insta-Gramme? We've heard it all before: 'Thou dost only posteth those pictures for attention!'

Ugh. Insecure knaves are the *worst*.

Convince him that you could never love another man the way you love him by suggesting a wild night of bedroom antics – so wild, in fact, that he'll need to use a cock ring. Fasten it onto his 'glorious manhood' (at least, that's what he thinks) so tightly that it loses blood circulation. Fingers crossed, gangrene will set in and it'll fall off.

DEATH BY
Cannon

ALL MEN DO is twitch in their sleep and lie, so next time he happens to be at war with the French, why not disguise yourself as one of his homies? (That armour is going to do WONDERS for your bum.)

Add an extra sprinkle of gunpowder to his favourite cannon, then stand back and watch the fireworks. After all, how were you supposed to know he'd be too close when it exploded?

DEATH BY

Pig

IMAGINE A MAN bragging about how many treasures he brought back from the Crusades, then making you pay for your own chicken leg at ye olde Kentucky Frye. Bloody unacceptable in any fool's language.

As he rides through the village, thinking he's the dog's bollocks, send a stray pig careering between his horse's legs. Incoming . . . a wealth of broken bones.

DEATH BY
Toe

WE ALL KNOW a Chad, don't we? A knave who is fond of punching walls – though, fortunately for him, ye olde wattle and daub isn't going to break his hand.

Rage bait him with casual, offhand remarks such as 'I really don't get what the big deal is – period pains are *way worse* than being elbowed in the balls!' (I mean . . . they are) and he might try a hefty kick instead. The joys of an infected toe and blood poisoning await.

DEATH BY
Cloak

THERE IS nothing worse than a man who brags about his conquests. So if you catch him telling everyone down the local tavern that he's known you in the biblical sense, you are perfectly within your right to shorten his lifespan.

Replace his favourite cloak with one that is a few inches longer. The unsuspecting manwench is bound to take a tumble . . . and never get up again.

DEATH BY
Fly

IF THERE'S one thing that gives me the ick, it's a man who gets loud and gropey after one too many pints of mead. But, as usual, it seems that Mother Nature is on our side. A fly in his tankard of ale truly would not go amiss.

Top tip: Why not try serenading him with a beautiful rendition of Sister Sabrina Carpenter's 'Manchild' on the lyre while he chokes to death?

DEATH BY
Apple

IF YOUR tarot cards have predicted that he is whatever the opposite of a munch is (nobody likes a selfish lover), I am afraid it is game over for your new boy toy.

Before he has the chance to accuse you of witchcraft (you did, after all, successfully predict that it would rain the other day when you put the washing out), inform him that it would be really sexy if he ate an apple while in the throes of lust. Hit him with ye olde 'But babe, if you shove the whole thing in your mouth, it acts as an aphrodisiac,' and because he's the sort of man who'd look up if you said the word 'gullible' was written on the ceiling, he will inevitably believe you.

Autoerotic asphyxiation with an apple . . . What a way to go.

DEATH BY

Horse and cart

IN THE EVENT of your boyfriend giving you the clap, no reaction is an overreaction.

Ask him to take you to ye olde Marke and Spencyr for some Percival Piglets (we love a passenger princess) and while he stands behind his cart to examine the ticket he received for parking on a double yellow line, give the horse a chance to stretch its neck by removing its harness.

If you've stopped on a slight hill, the cart will roll straight into him. Deserved, frankly.

DEATH BY
Colon

REMEMBER, ladies: if he insists upon going Dutch after he ate AN ENTIRE SWAN while you just picked at two chervil leaves and some pottage, he is not the man for you.

But worry not, for the swanky dinner will most likely leave him so constipated that he will die in agony on the toilet (he can have a nice little colon rupture, as a reward). He'll never think twice about picking up the bill again.

DEATH BY

Clutter

NOBODY LIKES a messy man. So if his gaff is littered with cow dung and empty tubes of Sir Pringalot's Stacked Wafers, you can try encouraging him to tidy it – but only after secreting a morning star among the mess.

Given his carelessness, he'll impale himself on the spikes.

DEATH BY

Tongue

IF HE TRIES to convince you that French and English are the same language, the man is a gaslighter extraordinaire. For this, however, there is a simple fix.

Debate him with such vigour that he bites his tongue in his haste to respond. Knowing his poor track record when it comes to dental hygiene (using honey as toothpaste? Be so for real, right now), it'll either fall off or a touch of blood poisoning will soon knock the wind out of his sails.

DEATH BY
Monkey

FOUND OUT your man has been moaning that you nag too much while he's tilling the fields with Brother Flavius? Of course his boysies are always going to have his back – he's one of *those* guys who makes everything he does about male validation, right down to having secret buxom girlfriends that he's too scared to introduce to his friends in case they tease him for being a 'chubby chaser'.

Convince him to purchase the latest exotic animal imported from lands afar to impress his boys and dress it up to match its new owner. The monkey will be so horrified, it'll bite him on sight.

DEATH BY
Fireplace

EVER DATED a guy who obsessively accuses you of cheating on him with Robin Hood? I have. And you know what? I wish I had.

After whispering sweet nothings in his ear to reassure him, coax him close to the fireplace for a romantic make-out sesh. So close, in fact, that his clothes catch fire.

Problem solved.

DEATH BY

Run

WHAT IS IT with twenty-eight-year-old men and getting really into marathon running? Like, I enjoy a jog through the cemetery as much as the next graverobber, but doing it in a paltock and tights does feel a little extra.

After he completes his next race, tell him you'll fancy him even more if he breaks the town record by running another lap. One swift heart attack later and he will never give you the ick again.

DEATH BY

Peeing

IF HE HAS an etching of him holding a fish on his ye olde Tyn'dre profile (or something along the lines of: '5'2 . . . Because apparently it matters'), you'd be doing womankind a favour by taking him out of the dating game. For good.

Why not invite him over for dinner? Get him drunk enough and when he gracefully excuses himself for a slash, inform him that your bog is located right on the edge of the battlements. Naturally, he'll believe you and he'll go flying.

DEATH BY
Whipped cream

NOTHING GIVES a girl the ick quite like a man who's more interested in his horse and cart than he is in her. If he spends more time polishing his wheels than he does satisfying your needs, he needs to GO.

So, when dusk falls, suggest introducing a touch of whipped cream in the bedroom and use it to stifle his senses: in his eyes, up his nose, in his ears, down his throat. Here's hoping it makes him short circuit.

DEATH BY

Astronomy

CALLING WOMEN 'females' unironically is a surefire way to irk the local maidens.

But hark! Fear not, damsels and baddies alike, for I am about to teach you how to gaslight, gatekeep and girlboss.

Lure him – I mean, invite him – on a moonlit stroll. When you see a shooting star, inform him that it is actually a comet and Judgement Day is upon us. Watch the man drop down dead from apoplexy, or panic and throw himself into a nearby river.

DEATH BY
Lightning

I HEAR YOUR boyfriend has been telling people that you're a witch? Ew. False accusations of heresy are *so* thirteenth-century.

Put his money where his mouth is and carve a little effigy of him out of a parsnip when the weather is looking ropey. Mutter some Latin under your breath, then send him outside to bring the washing in. With the help of Beelzebub himself (probably), he'll be struck by lightning.

DEATH BY
Tapestry

NOBODY WANTS to sleep with a man who doesn't clean his fingernails. That's a UTI just waiting to happen.

In the event of this disaster occurring, might I suggest rattling the bed frame with such vigour that the tapestry rod above your little love nest collapses, crushing him before any real damage can be done.

DEATH BY Prunes

HE WILL ONLY invite you to hang out for Scrollflix and chill *and* he expects you to pay ye olde Uber fare? Yuck! We expect nothing but princess treatment in the fourteenth century.

Next time you head over for your shameful little late-night rendezvous, bring a bottle of prune juice disguised as wine. He's the sort of greedy knave who'll drink the whole thing in one fell swoop, leaving him shitting his guts out until dehydration steals him from us.

DEATH BY

The bell

A MAN WHO adjusts his codpiece in public is – let's face it – probably a pervert. There's really no need for it, is there? Inform him that you love a charitable man who volunteers to ring the bells for the dead at your local church and then 'accidentally' tamper with the ropes a little.

You know the phrase 'saved by the bell'? Yeah, that'll be you when one of them comes loose and falls on his head.

DEATH BY

Well

IF YOU catch him liking random maidens' pictures on ye olde Insta-Gramme (particularly if they're clad solely in a wimple), you can wave that glorified court jester goodbye.

Inform him that the bracelet he gave you on your anniversary slipped off your wrist while you were collecting water from the local well. Little does he know that very well is rumoured to swallow sinners, so a perfectly timed 'BOO!' will send him tumbling straight into its murky depths, never to return.

DEATH BY Cesspit

AN UNEMPLOYED loser with no ambition is not the kind of boyfriend we yearn for in the fourteenth century, especially when he tries to convince you that the bale of hay on his bedroom floor is 'just temporary' while he tries to make it big as a ye olde SoundCloud chanter.

Instead of paying his bills, why not suggest he get a job as a gong farmer? They take anyone nowadays. Considering his inability to swim, he will inevitably drown in the very cesspit he's cleaning.

DEATH BY
Sweet tooth

SO YOU'RE telling me that this man finds a way to bring up his ex in EVERY conversation you two have? That emotionally unavailable knave doesn't deserve you, queen.

Next time your work husband brings you back some sugar from the latest Crusade, why not hire a professional confectioner to construct it into an edible statue of your vile boyfriend? When he scrans the lot, cavities, abscesses and eventual blood poisoning are guaranteed (and you can date your work husband instead. I do love a happy ending).

DEATH BY
Geese

HAVING a name that begins with the letter 'J' is an admission of guilt, in my opinion.

They've always got an ego the size of Windsor Castle, so it will come as no surprise to learn that if you get him drunk enough and challenge him to wrestle a gaggle of geese, he will comply. And better yet, the geese will win.

DEATH BY

Nosebleed

IF YOU'VE just tied the knot and you've caught him eyeing up the bridesmaids and imagining what they'd look like out of their kirtles, might I suggest pretending to trip over your own shoes and flailing your arms as much as possible, aiming for your new husband's nose? Choking to death on a nosebleed on his own wedding night seems highly appropriate, given the circumstances.

DEATH BY
Moat

MOST OF US have dated a man who wanders around with holes in his tights, particularly in the crotch area (thank God for the invention of the codpiece or his one-eyed womb ferret would be flapping in the wind). If you haven't, count yourself lucky.

When you're attending your next feast, offer to hold his goblet for him before 'accidentally' dropping it in the moat. He's the sort of fool who'll go diving straight in after it, and if a broken neck doesn't send him to Purgatory, drowning certainly will.

DEATH BY

Immurement

When he can't take rejection and instead hounds you with endless 'You up?' messages via carrier pigeon, the only option to quell his persistent tomfoolery is sudden death. Well. Not quite.

Invite him over for some 'Scrollflix and chill' (or, at least, that's what he thinks) when the builders have been doing renovation work at your place. Give him the old 'Yea, my bedchamber is just through there' and send him wandering into the very long, winding corridor that the workmen are just about to brick up.

The only downside is that bloke will be in your gaff forever, even if he is just a mouldy skeleton.

DEATH BY Peacock feathers

IF YOUR MAN'S creatine farts stink and he's constantly sketching mirror selfies while jousting with the boys, it may be safe to say that he's not really boyfriend material.

Next time he requests that you make him an insanely protein-dense dinner, opt for an ornate peacock pie. Just, y'know . . . forget to take the feathers out.

One of those lodged in his gullet will soon put a stop to his main character syndrome.

DEATH BY

Rat

MEN WHO aren't pet people are probably sociopaths. So if your horrid boyfriend refers to your cat as 'useless vermin', send Mr Kitty to stay with your sister and (nonchalantly) acquire a pet rat instead.

Train it to give him little playful nibbles on command and, as long sepsis doesn't kill him first, he will no doubt succumb to the plague. And you know what? This never would've happened if you'd had a cat in the house.

DEATH BY

Pie crust

A BLOKE LYING about having slain a dragon honestly screams itty bitty codpiece energy. He wants to be St George *so* badly.

So, next time you're invited to one of the king's banquets, convince your man to entertain your generous host by secreting himself inside a giant pie crust (rather than spinning those awful fabricated dits). Except – thanks to you overcooking the pastry slightly – he won't be able to break through it and yell 'SURPRISE!', leaving you with a very meaty (suffocated) man pie.

DEATH BY
Leather

IF YOU'VE discovered him liking an entire cache of incel videos on ye olde clock app, it's time for him to go.

Encourage him to seek work experience at his local tannery, and – somewhere along the line – mention in a rather offhand manner that bathing in pee is said to increase penis size. If he believes the utter rubbish he sees in these 'alpha male' sermons, of course he'll fall for that.

Rejoice, fair maiden, as he goes for a little dive in the enormous vat of urine the tanners use to cure leather, only to sink without a trace.

DEATH BY
Head

SO, HE DOESN'T say 'please' or 'thank you' to the tavern wench and sends the lamb stew he ordered back to the kitchen because he doesn't *actually* like lamb? Ew. Being rude to service staff is *so* ninth century.

Next time he rides valiantly into battle, tell him you'd love him to bring one of his slain enemies' heads home so you can pop it in the front garden like a decorative gnome. Undoubtedly, he will strap the decapitated skull to the side of his saddle and its teeth will nick his leg. The agonising throes of gangrene await.

DEATH BY

Gaslighting

DON'T TELL ME you *still* put up with your hideous boyfriend telling you to 'calm down' mid-argument?

The kindest thing to do in this situation is to convince him that he has some kind of deadly, flesh-eating rash on his back. Gaslight him so much that he develops a severe case of hypochondria and the stress should (hopefully) kill him.

DEATH BY
Horn

HE GHOSTED YOU? You're better off without that emotionally stunted popinjay anyway.

You know he goes hunting on Saturdays, so I suggest embellishing his usual patch of woodland with huge, fluttering red flags (because he is one, duh). This should utterly terrify his horse and he'll be bucked off, impaling himself – painfully, with any luck – on his bugle.

That'll be the last time you ever give him the raging horn.

DEATH BY

Gargoyle

THERE IS no excuse for a man peeing on the seat of the latrine. So, while I can't suggest potty-training a man in his thirties, I can recommend telling him to go do his business outside like a dog, seeing as he wants to behave like one. And wouldn't it be funny if a touch of grim weather made one of the gargoyles positioned oh-so-carefully on the battlements just . . . crumble away and land on his head?

DEATH BY
Tattoo

A MAN ASKING a woman if she's on her period *just because* she's asked him to do the washing-up twice should be a treasonable offence. (Who am I kidding? It should ALWAYS be a treasonable offence.)

Advise him to tattoo (carve) your name on his arm if he ever wants your forgiveness. Knowing how lazy he is, his dagger will be so rusty that his arm will likely end up falling off.

DEATH BY
Jousting

IF HE'S CONSTANTLY regurgitating manosphere crap ('Kneel not before a lass, lest thou be deemed a simp of the realm' and so forth), I beseech thee to inform him that he's not a real man unless he jousts with no armour on. His fragile male ego will only be too eager to comply and he'll be skewered like a spit-roasted hog at one of Henry III's banquets before you can say 'incel'.

DEATH BY
Ice skating

SPOTTED unwashed navy blue sheets and a flat pillow in your man's bedchamber?

Ask him to take you on a li'l ice skating date. Just, y'know, ignore the fact that the weather is getting warmer. Time it right and the ice will be so thin that he crashes straight into the freezing water below, never to be seen again.

(Bonus points if he falls over and you 'accidentally' skate over his fingers first.)

DEATH BY
Portcullis

IF THE WORDS 'But why don't you like me? Nice guys like me *never* get a chance, you females only date arseholes' ever leave his mouth, it's safe to say that it will be the last time he speaks to a woman.

Switch his cloak out for an extra-long one, and demand that he leave your home and never return. But as the gate begins to close, call out his name and he'll stop . . . And you can rejoice as his new cloak gets tangled in the portcullis and he is crushed to death.

DEATH BY Drawbridge

A KNAVE WHO plays ye olde video games until 1am while confidently ignoring his missus when she suggests he retires to the bedchamber with her clearly has a death wish. And you know what? Grant it to him.

When he inevitably pops outside to pick up his order from Sir Domino's Pye House (of course he didn't get you anything), 'accidentally' give the drawbridge winch a hearty tug. How were you to know he wouldn't move fast enough and end up squished against the gate?

DEATH BY
Cabbage soup

I THINK WE'VE all dated a man who utilises weaponised incompetence in an attempt to persuade you to mother him. As he can't be bothered to remember to dry-clean his codpiece or learn how to cook for himself, might I suggest making him soup from cabbages that have been lurking in the larder for at least two months? It'll be so rancid, he'll probably end up spewing up a kidney.

You'll never have to mother him again.

DEATH BY

Quicklime

IF HE DODGES his daily scrub with three-in-one body wash, shampoo and conditioner because the local physician has advised him that it will 'open his pores to miasma', I think he has a LOT more to worry about than a dose of sweating sickness.

Seeing as his personal hygiene is so lax, he probably won't notice you swap out his dry shampoo with quicklime. And because he's too lazy to *actually* wash his hair, of course he'll use it and burn his scalp clean off.

DEATH BY
Falcon

NOTHING SAYS 'inconsiderate manwench' quite like a bloke who tries to bonk you while you're having a menty b. It's even worse when he's dressed like a court jester (yeah, we've all been there).

Give him a pep talk about how you *really think* he could become a bird whisperer and encourage him to try it out on the king's falcon. Knowing him, he'll probably manage to say something offensive and the falcon will tear out his eyes.

DEATH BY
Song

THERE IS nothing more cringey than a man you matched with on ye olde Hynge announcing that he's written a song for you and then beginning to play the lute. You know damn well this heinous torture method has been used on many a maiden.

Alas, there is only one way to put a stop to his performative manwenchery for good. Flatter his musical skills enough and he'll try his best to out-sing the church choir, no doubt bursting a blood vessel and keeling over in the process.

DEATH BY

Reflection

IF HE HAS elected to acquire a set of ye olde Turkeye teeth and the most ridiculous bowl cut known to mankind (it's giving Magaluf final boss), it's probably time to call it quits, babe.

Lie like your life depends on it and tell him how scrumptious he looks. He'll spend so much time admiring himself in the reflection of his sword that he'll wander straight off the castle ramparts.

DEATH BY

Broken heart

HE DIDN'T send you an enormous bouquet of flowers or a swan statue sculpted out of sugar for the feast of Saint Valentine? FOR SHAME.

Dispatch your favourite page to his home with what the young'uns these days call 'a break-up text'. (Quite simple, really: 'Oi, knobhead. It's over.') He'll be so gutted – because, obviously, you're great – that a broken heart will send him straight to the gates of Hell. Even Satan himself will be standing there, shaking his head: 'You didn't get her anything for Valentine's, mate? Rookie move.'

After all, it's where he belongs.

GLOSSARY

CODPIECE – A pouch designed to hold a man's genitals so we don't see any low-hanging fruit peeking out from under his paltock (and to gaslight us into thinking his junk is bigger than it actually is).

CUCKING/DUCKING STOOL – Dishonest tradesmen, naggy women, and accused witches would be tied to this stool and dunked in water repeatedly to either force a confession or to test their guilt.

CUNNY – A slightly less vulgar version of the c-word used to refer to a woman's genitals.

GONG FARMER – A man whose job entails digging waste out of privies and cesspits. Not exactly the sexiest line of employment...

JOUSTING – A medieval sporting pastime involving two armoured men brandishing lances and charging at one another on horseback.

KIRTLE – A close-fitting medieval gown designed to provide support for the bust (how did we actually survive without bras?) and shape the silhouette.

KNAVE – A dishonest man (often substituted for 'lying arsehole' in the modern day).

LAMPREYS – A medieval delicacy that looks like something straight out of a horror film. Sometimes known as 'vampire fish', they are bizarre little creatures which resemble an eel. Their sucker-like mouths are filled with razor-sharp teeth.

MORNING STAR – A medieval weapon embellished with spikes.

PALTOCK – A men's tunic. These kept getting shorter and shorter as the Middle Ages wore on, leading to the invention of the codpiece to avoid instances of indecent exposure.

POPINJAY – A vain man (likely with narcissistic tendencies).

POTTAGE – A thick soup cooked in a cauldron over the hearth. Because it was constantly kept on the fire with ingredients added over time, parts of it could end up being weeks or months old.

WENCH – A medieval term for a young woman or girl.

Born and raised in London, Megan's first love was her glorious city and its morbid past. A prolific writer and keen historian, she has been interviewed on BBC Radio London and featured in national publications including the *Mirror* and the *Express*. She graduated with a First Class Bachelor's Degree with Honours in History from Queen Mary University of London in 2021, followed by a Masters degree in History four years later. You can find Megan on TikTok (@historyoflondon), where she blends her love of the metropolis with tales of crime, scandal, and the paranormal. She is the author of the self-published *A Ghostly Guide to London*, and now leads her own history tours across the city.